Oxford Primary Social Studies

Living Together

Pat Lunt

2

OXFORD
UNIVERSITY PRESS

Contents

1 Family and culture

In this unit you will learn:
- what it means to be part of a family
- about other sorts of groups
- to celebrate the differences between people and their cultures
- to work together in a group.

? Which special celebrations do you have in your family?

traditional   marriage
culture   heritage   goal
ingredients

1.1 My place in my family

In these lessons you will learn:
- what makes a family
- that we have different relationships within our family.

Families

When we speak of a family we sometimes mean a group of people made up of only parents and their children. The size of this family can vary, depending on how many children the parents have.

The children in these families are brothers and sisters to each other and are sons or daughters to the parents.

The word 'family' also means other relations beyond parents and their children. This wider family includes relatives such as grandparents, aunts, uncles and cousins.

▲ In some countries it is common for many family members to live together in the same house or very close by.

People in a family are special

All of the people in our family are special to us. They are the ones who love and care for us.

In our family we learn how to show respect. We learn to live together, to share and to help one another.

Our brothers and sisters can help us learn to share and how to play together well.

▲ Older brothers and sisters can help with raising younger children.

Sometimes members of our wider family will help to look after us.

Activities

1 Make a drawing showing you, the family members who share your home, and other family members.

2 Write about your relationship with three different members of your family.

1.2 Together as a family

In this lesson you will learn:
- what is good about spending time with our family
- to say how a family spends time together.

The importance of family

Families are important.

We say we are 'part of a family' because we belong there. Each member of the family helps to make it what it is.

We should feel safe and loved in our family.

We can share all our cares and worries with people in our family.

We can share all our joys and successes as well.

Family time

We have very special relationships with members of our family. For any relationship to grow, the people in that relationship need to spend time together. This is true for families too.

◀ There are some times in the day when family members can all be together.

▲ Our family can help us as we learn.

When family members spend time together they get to know each other really well.

In a family we learn how to co-operate and how to share. We learn about showing respect and treating people well.

◀ Families sometimes share special outings.

Activities

1 Work in a small group to talk and write about things a family does together.

2 Write down what you think people learn during these times and what they enjoy.

In these lessons you will learn:
○ why it is good to be in a family.

Basic human needs

We all have basic needs.

We need water, food, clothing and shelter. We call these our physical needs. They are things our body needs in order to survive.

We also need love and friendship. These are some of our emotional needs.

The family and our physical needs

Babies cannot do anything for themselves.
They rely on others to provide for all their needs.

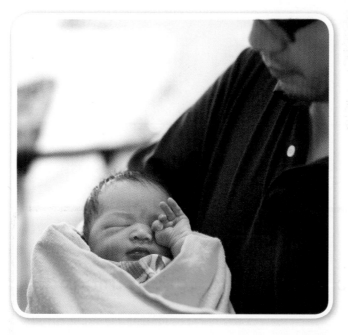

◀ When babies are born they are completely helpless.

As children grow they can do more things for themselves but they still need a family to provide things like food, clothes and shelter.

Parents are usually responsible for providing these. Parents also make sure that children get an education and any medical care they need.

◀ Which physical need is this person providing for?

The family and our emotional needs

People need to feel loved and cared for. They need encouragement.

Family members should get these things from each other.

We should feel safe within a family and able to tell others how we are feeling.

▲ Parents can help and encourage their children in many ways.

Activities

1 Write about how your family meets your physical needs.

2 Work in a group to make up role plays that show when a child might need to feel love, care or encouragement.

1.4 Family celebrations

In this lesson you will learn:
- about different family celebrations
- that family celebrations are an important part of a country's culture
- that family celebrations are an important part of a group's culture
- that family celebrations are not the same in all countries or groups.

Family celebrations

We celebrate when we are happy about something or when we want to mark an event in a special way.

Traditional family celebrations include special occasions such as the birth of a baby or a **marriage**.

In many **cultures** it is usual to celebrate a person's birthday each year.

Births

The birth of a new baby is a very special occasion for a family. It is a joy to the mother and the father. Other family members can celebrate because there is happiness that the family has a new member.

▲ A new life is always a cause for celebration.

Marriages

Celebrating a marriage is important because it marks a special point in the relationship between two people. The married couple will go on from this point to make their own home and perhaps start their own family.

Celebrations and culture

Family celebrations are an important part of the culture in which the family lives. Celebrations often include special food and people wear special clothes which are also important in the family's culture.

▲ Kwanzaa is a family celebration kept by African families around the world.

▲ Chinese families all around the world celebrate Chinese New Year.

Activity

Make an invitation card inviting someone to a special celebration in your family. The card should explain the reason for the celebration, say what will be happening, what food there will be and if guests need to wear any special clothes.

1.5 Groups

Groups

We spend a lot of time in different groups of people. These include our family, our friends, our class and our school.

In all these groups we do different things together.

Each group gives us different things.

We behave differently in each group.

The family group

Our family is one of the closest groups we have. The family provides food and clothes. It also provides love, care and support.

There are special ways of behaving in the family and there may be some rules to follow. For example, we will be expected to show respect to people in the group.

Friendship groups

Another close group is made up of our friends.

Friends enjoy the same sort of things.

Our friends support us and help us to feel good about ourselves.

We hope our friends will be kind and loyal.

◄ Personal relationships are very important in friendship groups.

Class and school groups

In class and school we learn to live alongside other people. We learn to co-operate.

There are class and school rules about behaviour that we need to follow.

▲ In school we learn to live alongside many other people.

Activities

1 Write about your friendship groups, what you like about them and how to be a good friend.

2 Make a poster that explains how to be a good member of the class.

1.6 Activity groups

In this lesson you will learn:
- to identify the different organised groups to which you belong
- to say what behaviour is expected in each group
- to say what is good about being in these groups.

Organised groups

We sometimes belong to groups because we want to do a particular thing.

We can play a sport we enjoy.

We can share our interests.

We can do things for other people or for the environment.

> **Did you know?**
> The first Scout troops were formed in the UK in 1907 and today there are an estimated 28 million scouts around the world and 10 million girl guides and girl scouts.

▲ We sometimes join a group to do something we enjoy.

Behaviour in organised groups

There is usually a leader in an organised group.

We need to respect leaders and listen carefully to instructions.

The leader may be helping us to learn new skills or explaining something we need to know.

There is often a **goal** that we share with other people in the group.

To meet this goal we must learn to co-operate.

? What are some goals of different activity groups?

◀ There are many chances to work together in a group.

What do organised groups offer?

In an organised group we can learn and practise new skills.

We can do something we enjoy with people who have the same interest.

We can learn to work together as a team.

We have a sense of belonging to the group. It becomes part of who we are.

Activity

Write about some of the organised groups you belong to in and out of school.

1.7 Personal qualities

In these lessons you will learn:
- to identify different personal qualities
- to recognise that people have different personal qualities
- to say why positive personal qualities are good.

Personal qualities

We are different in many ways.

▲ We do not all look the same.

▲ We do not all like the same things or act the same way.

We also have different personal qualities.

These qualities make us think, feel and react in different ways.

Different kinds of personal qualities

Some personal qualities are helpful. These make us feel good about ourselves and help us get on well with other people.

Some personal qualities can be less helpful. These are parts of ourselves that we feel less good about. They are things about ourselves that we know it would be good to change.

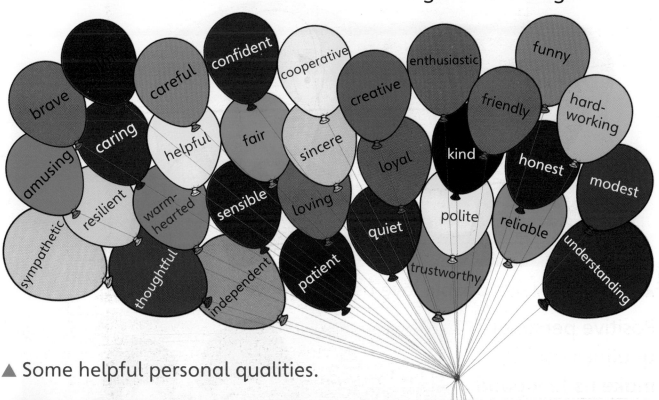

▲ Some helpful personal qualities.

Activities

1 Talk with a partner about the helpful personal qualities shown in the illustration. Copy any words that you do not understand.

2 Copy this sentence; 'If you are … it means you …' Fill in the spaces with a personal quality from the list and explain what it means. Do this for five different words.

1.8 Celebrating positive qualities

In this lesson you will learn:

- ○ to identify positive personal qualities
- ○ to say which personal qualities you have
- ○ to say which personal qualities other people have.

Seeing good qualities

▲ It is good when people love us for who we are.

Positive personal qualities usually make us feel good about ourselves.

It is good to think that we can be kind or thoughtful.

▲ There are many times when we can be kind or helpful.

It is good to feel confident and happy to try out new things.

We do not always know which personal qualities we have.

It is helpful when other people say they can see good qualities in us.

It is helpful to tell other people the good things we can see in them.

We can tell people when we think they have been kind, congratulate them when they have done something well and encourage them when they have faced a challenge.

▲ We face challenges every day.

Activities

1 Make a list of good things you can say about yourself. Think about:
   - how you behave with your family and friends – are you kind, considerate, helpful, loyal?
   - your work in school – are you hard-working, determined?
   - other things you like to do – are you confident, co-operative, enthusiastic?

2 Make a decorated shape with your name on. Add a positive personal quality you think you have. Let other people in the class add positive personal qualities to your name shape.

3 Think about a person who is special to you and write about what makes them special.

In these lessons you will learn:

- that people wear different clothes in different places
- that traditional clothes are a part of culture
- that everyone's traditions and cultures should be respected.

Clothes

People have different ways of deciding what to wear.

? How do you decide what to wear? Does it depend on what you are going to do?

▲ Sometimes we wear a special uniform to show that we belong to a group.

Traditional clothes

Traditional clothes are very different around the world.

People wear traditional clothes to show that they belong to a certain group or tribe.

▲ These people live in Africa. Their clothes help to protect them from the sun. What are the similarities and differences between the clothes shown on these pages?

▲ These children are from Norway where it is sometimes very cold. There are traditional patterns on the clothes.

People's traditional dress is very special to them. It is part of their culture.

◀ Some traditional clothes look very special.

Activities

1 Draw a picture of the clothes you would wear to relax and the clothes you would wear to a special occasion.

2 Design some clothing that shows some of the things and ideas that are important to you.

1.10 Homes in different places

In these lessons you will learn:

- that people from different places have different homes
- that traditional homes are a part of culture
- that everyone's traditions and cultures should be respected.

A place to live

People have traditionally made their homes from the materials that were available nearby.

Did you know?

In many traditional societies where people live on the coast or by a river, people build their houses raised above the water on tall legs called stilts.

▲ People in places with plenty of trees made their homes from wood.

Materials for making homes include wood, stone, straw, rushes and reeds, animal skins, mud, bricks and even ice and snow!

▲ Houses made from straw.

▲ A home that is made from fabric.

◀ Building flats one on top of the other means that lots of people can live in the same place, without taking up too much space on the ground.

Many houses today are made from **concrete**, **steel** and glass.

Homes are special

Whatever a home looks like, it is a special place. It is where people can shelter from the weather. It is where a family lives together.

Activity

Work in a group to draw an imaginary place where you are going to build a settlement.

- Think what materials will be available for you to build homes. Draw what some of these homes will look like.

- Write about how they will provide for all the needs of the people who live in this place.

1.11 Food in different places

In these lessons you will learn:
- that people from different places enjoy different food
- that traditional foods are a part of culture
- that everyone's traditions and cultures should be respected.

Food in different places

In the past, people always settled in places where they could find all the things they would need. They would need material to make clothes and houses. They would need water to drink and food to eat. The food would be different depending on where they lived.

▲ People who lived near a river or by the sea would catch fish from the water.

▲ People who settled as farmers would grow crops and keep animals to provide some of their food.

Traditional food

Over time, particular dishes of food, made from local **ingredients**, have become an important part of a country's culture and **heritage**. These dishes are sometimes known as the 'National Dish' of that country.

These foods have particular meaning for the people who eat them. The food is part of the way they know that they belong to a particular group or to a particular place.

▲ National dishes from around the world can look very different.

Food from around the world may look very different but it reminds us of one thing we share: we all need to eat.

Activities

1 Draw and label pictures of five foods and a picture of your favourite food dish.

2 Draw and write about the national dish from your country and one other.

Unit 1 Review questions

1 Being in a family helps us:
   a run faster
   b learn about showing care and respect
   c tell the time
   d learn about the environment

2 When people hold a celebration they are:
   a sorry for something they have done wrong
   b practising a new skill
   c happy about an event and want to mark it in a special way
   d sad because they have lost something special

3 The members of an organised group often share the same goal. This is:
   a the way they score points
   b a uniform they need to wear
   c a skill they want to learn
   d what they hope the group will achieve

4 Write about three things you do with your family and what you enjoy about these times.

5 Describe two ways in which your family helps to care for your body and helps you to feel good.

6 Write about three things you might see or hear as part of a celebration.

7 Write about a group you belong to. Explain what happens in the group and say what you enjoy.

8 Think about a time when you helped someone. What did you do and how did it make you feel?

 2 History and heritage

In these lessons you will learn:
- about generations in a family
- to use and draw a timeline
- about things that change during a person's lifetime
- to draw a family tree and a timeline.

generation   timeline
technology
gadget   family tree

? How and why do things change over time?

27

2.1 A simple family tree

In this lesson you will learn:
- that families are made up of different generations
- how to show your family on a family tree.

Different generations

Families are made up of different **generations**.

Children are from one generation. Their parents are from another.

A child has a mother and father. They are that child's parents.

The parents' mothers and fathers are the child's grandparents.

▲ Three generations of a family – children, parents and grandparents.

A family tree

A family tree is a way of showing how people in a family are related to each other.

In the drawing of a family tree you can see leaves around the top labelled 'brother' and 'sister'. These are all the children in a family.

Moving down the tree are two leaves, one on each side of the tree. One is for these children's mother and one is for their father.

At the bottom of the tree are leaves for grandmothers and grandfathers. The leaves for the mother and her parents are on the same side of the tree and leaves for the father and his parents are on the other.

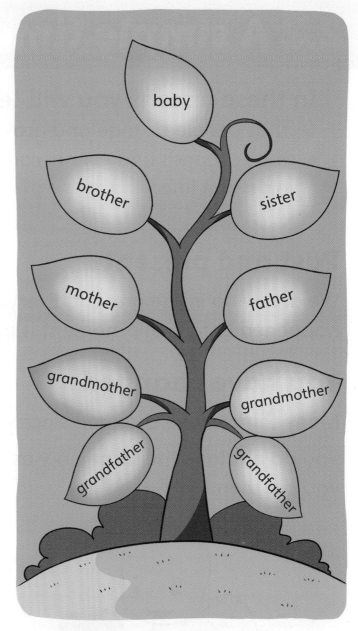

▲ A simple family tree.

Activity

Make a family tree that shows you and any brothers or sisters you have, your parents and your grandparents. Can you think of any other family members who you could add to your tree?

2.2 A simple timeline

In these lessons you will learn:
- that people change and grow over time
- that changes and events can be shown on a timeline.

Past and present

We are living in the present. Everything that has happened before this moment is in the past.

You have changed

Many things have changed since you were a baby.

You do not look the same now as you did then.

▲ You do not wear the same clothes as you did when you were a baby.

▲ You don't sleep in the same kind of bed as a baby.

◀ You do not play with baby toys.

A simple timeline

What sort of things have happened since you were a baby?

You may have moved house. You may have got younger brothers and sisters.

You may have gone to a play group or kindergarten before starting school.

We can use a special diagram, called a **timeline**, to show the order in which things have happened.

▲ This simple timeline shows some of the things that have happened since Samya was born.

Activities

1 Draw and label a picture of you as a baby and the things you may have worn, slept in or played with. Then draw and label a picture of yourself and the things you wear, sleep in and play with today.

2 Write about three things that have changed about you and the things you can do.

3 Draw a simple timeline like the one in this book. Write and draw things that have happened in your life. Make sure you put them in the correct order.

2.3 A family timeline

In these lessons you will learn:

- that families change and grow over time
- how to write questions for historical research
- how to show changes and events on a timeline.

Changes in the family

Lots of changes happen in a family as time passes.

The number of people in a family can get larger.

▲ A baby adds a new member to a family.

The number of people living in the household can get smaller.

Family members might move away to attend a university or for work. When younger family members are old enough they leave the household to live in their own home.

◀ When people get married they move away and might start a family of their own.

Another big change is when a family moves to live in a new place.

A family timeline

To make a timeline for your family you need to know things that have happened in your family since you were born, and also before you were born.

▲ Families move to new places for many reasons.

Activity

Work with a partner to think of some questions you could ask family members to find out the information you need for your timeline. These are some of the things that you need to find out:

- when your parents were born
- where they lived when they were children
- when they married
- how long they have lived in the home they live in now
- when your grandparents were born
- where your grandparents lived.

2.4 Changes in a lifetime

In these lessons you will learn:
- about changes that happen during a person's lifetime.

The environment changes

Some changes in the natural environment happen so slowly that we are not really aware of them. Changes that are a result of human activity can happen much faster. Areas might be cleared for farming or building. Settlements change in size.

▲ What might be similar and what might be different for people living in these two places?

Changes in transport

The way people travel changes. Many people travel by car, coach, bus and train. Goods and raw materials are transported within countries and around the world.

▲ Today, people can travel quickly between countries.

◄ Ships like this are constantly taking goods around the world.

Changes in communication

Today we can communicate with people all around the world. We can see pictures of events as they happen from almost anywhere in the world.

Changes in the home

Technology is making a very big difference to lots of people's lives.

Today people have many **gadgets** around the house.

◀ Some gadgets are to help with running the household and some are just for fun. Some can be used for both.

Think how your life would be different if there was no electricity.

Activities

1 Make a labelled drawing of all the things in your living room at home and all the things in your bedroom. Mark off the ones you think would not have been in your parents' living room and bedroom when they were children.

2 Write about some big changes that have happened in the environment, transport, communication and homes.

Unit 2 Review questions

1 In a family, people from different generations are:
   a brothers and sisters
   b aunts and uncles
   c children, parents and grandparents
   d the families of married couples

2 A timeline is a diagram that:
   a helps us to tell the time
   b shows things that happen in the order of time
   c shows how many times something happens
   d shows what happens during the day

3 Which of these lists shows the correct order in which these things were invented?
   a Car, horse and cart, aeroplane
   b Aeroplane, car, horse and cart
   c Horse and cart, aeroplane, car
   d Horse and cart, car, aeroplane

4 When science is used to help in business or in the home this is called:
   a being inventive
   b creativity
   c technology
   d designing

5 Draw a simple diagram that shows three generations of one family.

6 Write about two things that have happened to you since you were a baby.

7 Write about two important things that have happened in your family in the last three years.

8 Suggest two ways you think the place where you live has changed in the last ten years.

9 Explain how modern ships and modern aeroplanes make a difference to the way people and goods are moved today.

10 Explain how three gadgets in your home are used and who uses them.

3 People and places

In this unit you will learn:

- how to use different types of maps and keys
- how to use a globe
- about the different things we describe as 'weather'
- about the importance of water
- to keep a weather record
- to prepare a presentation.

symbol
built-up   continent
industry   key

? How do globes and maps help us to find out about the world?

3.1 A local map

In these lessons you will learn:
- how to use a local map
- to find things on a local map
- to say where things are in relation to each other on a map
- how to use directions on a map.

What is a map?

▲ What is this child doing?

Maps are a special picture of what is on the ground in real life.

All the things shown on a map are drawn as if you were looking straight down on them. They are also shown in a very simple way.

A map will show roads, important buildings and parks as well as natural features such as beaches or hills.

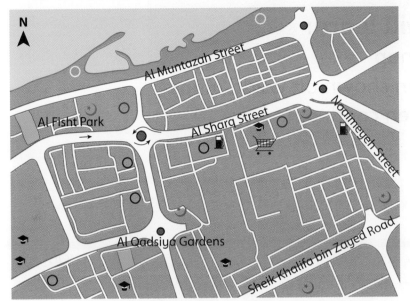

Key
🕓 Mosque   🛢 Petrol station
○ Holiday resort   ○ Police station
🏫 School   ▬ Public park and garden
○ Restaurant   🛒 Shopping mall

◀ This local map shows a **built-up** area where there are homes, schools, shops and parks.

A map helps us to see where things are in relation to each other. We can see if two places are close together or far away.

We can find out ways of getting between one place and another.

The map also has a **key**. This tells you what the **symbols** on the map mean.

Activities

1 Use the map and the key to answer these questions.

- How many schools are shown on the map?
- What colour are parks and gardens on the map?
- Which park is close to a school?
- What does Al Muntazah Street run beside?

2 With a friend, discuss the route between the two parks.

3.2 A world map

In this lesson you will learn:

- how to use a world map
- about the information shown on world maps
- the names of the seven continents.

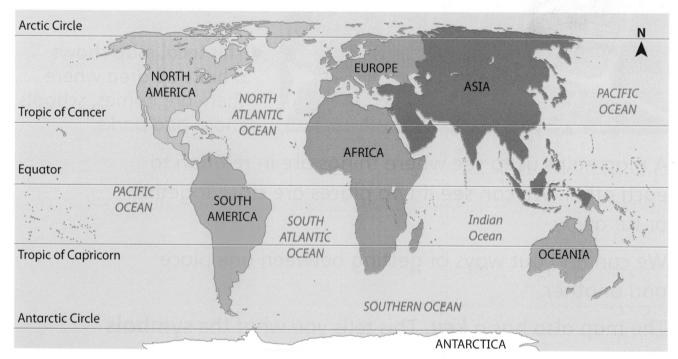

▲ This map shows the continents and oceans of the world.

Continents

The land of the world is divided up into large areas known as **continents**.

The continents are Asia, Africa, North America, South America, Antarctica, Europe and Australasia.

Apart from Antarctica, each continent has many different countries within it.

Useful information

The map on this page shows the equator and the Arctic and Antarctic Circles. These lines help us to say where things are on the Earth.

We can talk about places being north or south of the equator.

We can say that a place is north or south of the Arctic Circle or Antarctic Circle.

Activity

Use the map to answer these questions.

1 Which continents have some of their land south of the equator?

2 Which continents have some of their land above the Arctic Circle?

3 Which continents join to Asia on the west?

4 Which continent is between the South Atlantic Ocean and the Indian Ocean?

3.3 World maps and globes

In these lessons you will learn:

- how to find countries on a world map and globe
- about the information shown on world maps.

A country is an area of land that has definite borders. The land inside the borders makes up the country. Everything inside the borders belongs to the country.

There are nearly 200 separate countries in the world.

▲ These images help us to see the shape of the world. A **globe** makes this even clearer.

Talking about continents and countries helps us to locate places in the world. We can say, for example, that the country of Egypt is in the continent of Africa.

▲ This globe clearly shows the continents of Africa and Europe

▲ This globe clearly shows the continent of Asia

Activity

Work in a group to locate the country in which you are now living and five more you know of on a world map and a globe. Look at the world map on page 40 to help you find which continent each one is in.

3.4 What is the weather?

In these lessons you will learn:
- about what makes up the weather
- to keep a record of the weather.

The weather is made up of a number of different things.

Sunshine

The sun shines during the day.

The sun rises early in the morning. It is low in the sky and it is not very strong.

As the day goes on the sun seems to rise in the sky and it feels stronger.

Late in the afternoon and into the evening the sun sinks and becomes weaker.

▲ The sun feels weaker when it is setting.

Wind

When a lot of air moves we call it a wind. The wind blows from different directions and at different strengths.

◀ When the wind blows we can fly kites.

Temperature

The temperature in weather is how hot or cold the air is. The air is warmed by the sun. How hot or cold we feel depends on the temperature of the air.

Precipitation

Precipitation is the word used to describe anything that falls from clouds. It includes rain, hailstones and snow.

▲ Rain is good for growing crops.   ▲ Heavy rain can cause many problems.

Clouds

Clouds are made of water droplets. Clouds form in the sky. Sometimes they block the sun. Sometimes they bring rain or snow.

> **Did you know?**
> The place that gets the most rainfall in a year is Mawsynram in India where 11 873 mm (467 in) of rain falls every year. Most of it falls between June and September.

Activities

1 Make a chart of symbols that show the different parts of weather.

2 Keep a record for a week of the weather in your country and in another, distant country. How is it the same and how is it different?

3.5 Water for life

Where we find water

Water is a natural resource which means that it is found in nature. Water is naturally stored in rivers, lakes and oceans and in the ground.

When we use water we take it from these natural stores. It takes a long time for the stores to fill up again.

Living things and water

All living things need water in order to survive and so we have to remember that it is a very precious resource.

▲ Some animals eat plants for food. The plants need water. The animals must drink water too.

Using water wisely

We use water in many ways.

We use it in our homes to clean, cook and wash ourselves.
We use water to wash dishes, clothes and cars.

It is used in **industry** in many ways.

It is used by farmers for animals and to water crops.

▲ Plants in a garden need to be watered.

◀ Watering crops uses a lot of water.

It is sometimes hard to find enough water for all our needs, especially in places where it is hot and dry.

We should never waste water.

Activities

1 Talk with a friend about all the ways in which water is used by people, animals and plants and then write about one each of these.

2 Work in a group to give a presentation that explains how water is used in the home and how to avoid wasting water.

Unit 3 Review questions

1 A special drawing of the things on the surface of the Earth is called:
   a a painting
   b a collage
   c a design
   d a map

2 If there is one direction arrow on a map this shows:
   a north
   b south
   c east
   d west

3 The symbols used on a map are explained in a:
   a compass rose
   b colour code
   c key
   d scale

4 The land on the Earth is divided into seven large areas known as:
   a countries
   b continents
   c oceans
   d physical features

5 The heat from the sun feels:
   a the same all day
   b strongest in the middle of the day
   c strongest at sunset
   d strongest at sunrise

6 Water is stored naturally in:
   a rivers, lakes and bottles
   b lakes, rivers and buckets
   c rivers, lakes and oceans
   d lakes, tanks and oceans

7 Write about two ways in which people can use maps.

8 Write two things that might be shown on a map of the world.

9 Explain one difference between a map and a globe.

10 Write two things you could say about the weather today.

11 Give two reasons why water is so important.

12 Write two ways you have used water today.

4 Citizenship

In this unit you will learn:

- about your responsibilities
- how to behave well
- how to care for the environment
- how to re-use some waste items
- how to manage your money.

? What can you do to help look after our planet?

society

contribution   manners

landfill site   polluted

responsibilities

In these lessons you will learn:
- the difference between needs, wants and rights
- that rights come with responsibilities
- the responsibilities and rights you have at home.

Responsibilities in the home

The family is at the heart of the community.

Everyone has certain **responsibilities** in the family and in the home. These responsibilities are to do with making sure that the home is a safe, happy and peaceful place.

Parents have a responsibility to provide for the physical and emotional needs of their children.

Parents must ensure their children receive any medical care they need.

Parents should make sure that their children have the opportunity to be educated.

Parents should teach children about the behaviour that is expected of them in **society**.

◀ Children learn the correct way to behave in the home.

Children have a responsibility not to waste or spoil any of the things provided for them.

Children should obey household rules.

Children should show respect and care towards other family members.

Children's rights in the home

Children should get all they need to feel happy and respected and to be healthy.

Children should receive any medical care they need.

Children should be kept safe and be taught about staying safe.

▲ A child's health is very important.

▲ Children are happy when they know they are loved.

Activities

1 Draw and write about the responsibilities of two different people within a home.

2 Work in a group and write some rules you would have about keeping safe in the home.

4.2 What I should do at school

In this lesson you will learn:

- the responsibilities and rights you have at school.

Responsibilities in school

Many different people work in a school. The head teacher and all the teaching staff help children to learn. There are people who work as receptionists and secretaries. A school also has a school nurse, cooks and caretakers.

▲ The people in a school have different roles and responsibilities.

Each person in school has a duty to attend for their hours of work and to perform all their tasks as well as they can.

Students' responsibilities

Students have responsibilities in school too.

Students should ensure that they attend school and work hard.

Students' behaviour around school should ensure everyone stays safe.

Students should obey all class and school rules.

Students should not waste or damage any of the things given to them to use.

▲ School equipment should be treated carefully.

Rights in school

Everyone in school has the right to be treated with respect.

Everyone in school has the right to feel safe.

Children have a right to be educated.

▲ Good classroom behaviour shows respect for everybody.

Activity

Work in a small group to make a poster of a student's right or a student's responsibility in school.

In these lessons you will learn:

- that you can always make choices
- how you are responsible for your own choices and actions
- some good habits of behaviour
- about self-discipline.

Rules and personal choices

All groups of people have rules.

People are still responsible for the choices they make.

The important thing is to make good choices.

▲ What is a good choice to make here?

Rules help us make good choices

Rules help us to think about what is good for us and for others.

Following rules means we behave in ways that make sure that everyone gets the most out of a situation, is happy and feels safe.

We may need rules to begin with, to help us practise behaving in a certain way. After a while, we behave in that way without the rule. It is as if the rule has become part of us. For example, we do not need a rule to tell us that it is better to be kind to another person than to be unkind.

Self-discipline

This means that we control our emotions and actions. We do not simply react to things.

We also need self-discipline to achieve certain things, like learning a particular skill.

▲ If we want to learn a special skill then we have to practise.

Activities

1 Write about some situations where you can choose to do the right thing.

2 Talk with a partner and write about times when you have to practise self-discipline.

4.4 What I should do for others

In this lesson you will learn:
- about belonging to different groups
- how to behave in different groups
- about responsibilities you have to other people in the group.

We belong to different groups

We often think about what we want and what we need.

When we are in a group we must remember that other people in the group have things they want and need as well. We should behave in a way that makes sure other people sometimes get what they want and need.

This helps everyone enjoy being in the group. This is part of our responsibility towards these other people.

▲ We all belong to different groups.

Responsibilities in different groups

People need and want different things from different groups.

In our family people want to know they are cared for. We must make sure our behaviour does not upset anyone or make anybody in the family unhappy.

Some groups have a special purpose or **aim**. In these groups people need to work together to help achieve those aims.

▲ Lots of people have to work together on a new building.

Activity

Talk with a friend and write about a group to which you belong:

- Decide if the group has a special aim or goal.

- Decide what people in the group want and need.

- Think how group members can make sure the group's aims, and people's wants and needs, are met.

4.5 Making a difference

In these lessons you will learn:
- about belonging to different groups
- about responsibilities you have in different groups
- about the contribution you can make to the groups.

Playing a part

People in a group often have a special aim or goal. In a sports team this might be winning a game or a trophy. In school it might simply be making the classroom a happy place where people can learn.

Everybody in these groups has a part to play in reaching their goal. When this happens we say that everyone has made a **contribution**.

▲ Sometimes everyone must play their part in order to achieve the goal!

Different contributions

Sometimes it is easy to know what contribution we can make. If there is a time of working in a group in school then everybody has to work together and co-operate. People in the group will perhaps be given different jobs. Each person makes a contribution that helps finish the task.

Working together well in a group helps the class be a happy place where everyone can work.

▲ How are these children contributing to the class?

Activities

1 Work in a group and write about all the ways in which students can contribute to the class.

2 Write about another group to which you belong. Explain what contribution you make to that group.

4.6 Rules and behaviour

In these lessons you will learn:
- to explain the reasons for having rules
- to say how your behaviour changes in different situations.

Living by the rules

We can all do so many different things.

Some things we can do on our own and in our own way.

Some things we do together. When we do things together we have to behave in a certain way.

▲ When we create a picture we can decide what it will look like on our own.

▲ When we sing together we all have to sing the same tune.

▲ We cannot play a game together if we are following different rules.

Rules in society

We expect people to behave in certain ways in society. There are no written rules, and people get to know about this usually from their parents and places like school.

There are other rules, called laws, that are written down and which are about particular types of behaviour. They let people know the things they should do and things they must not do.

▲ There are sometimes rules that tell us how to behave in certain places.

Many rules are there to keep order and to help people stay safe.

Obeying such rules and laws shows that we want to help keep order and help people to stay safe.

Activities

1 Talk in a group about three different places where there are rules to follow. Decide what the rules are for and be ready to tell the class.

2 Work in a group to invent a village or an island. Decide who will live there, what people will do and what rules there will be to keep the community happy and safe.

4.7 Polite behaviour

In this lesson you will learn:
- to identify behaviour that is expected in school and in public.

Our parents and family teach us how to behave well with others. This behaviour is known as our **manners**.

Polite things to say

When we ask for something we say 'Please'. When we are given something we say 'Thank you'.

When we meet someone we greet them, perhaps by saying 'Hello.' When we leave someone we say a farewell, perhaps by saying 'Goodbye'.

When we want to go past someone or we need to get their attention we say 'Excuse me'.

If we do something wrong or upset someone we say 'I'm sorry.'

▲ If we do something by accident, it is still good manners to say 'Sorry'.

> **Did you know?**
>
> In many cultures it is polite to eat everything on your plate. It lets people know you have enjoyed the food. In other cultures it is polite to leave a little food on your plate. This shows your hosts that they have given you enough to eat.

Polite things to do

We can hold a door open for someone and let them through.

We wait for our turn, whether in a line or waiting to speak.

If other people are speaking or busy working we are quiet.

We cover our mouth if we cough or sneeze.

▲ It is polite to offer to help other people.

Polite ways to eat

You should not put too much food into your mouth at once.

You should not speak when you are chewing food.

You should not eat too quickly.

Activities

1 In a group, make a list of ways in which you can be polite in school and in public.

2 Make up some role plays that show people using good manners.

4.8 Other people's property

In these lessons you will learn:
- how we should treat other people's property
- how we should treat shared property.

People's private property

We all have things that belong to us. We say this is our 'private property'.

Some of the things we have are special to us.

We do not want anyone to damage our things.

We do not want anyone to take our things without our permission.

▲ We should always treat another person's things with care.

Looking after shared things

Sometimes we share things with other people. These things do not belong to us but they belong to everybody.

We share the chairs, tables and all the equipment in the classroom.

▲ Why should we look after the things a school provides for us?

We share the playground and other open spaces in the school.

There are parks and other public places in the community.

We need to look after all these things and places.

Activities

1 Discuss with a friend something you have which is very special to you. Explain how you would feel if it was damaged or broken.

2 Work in a group to design and label a public park. Make a sign that asks people to look after the park.

4.9 My local area

In this lesson you will learn:
- about human activity in the local area
- to say how this activity affects the environment.

Human activity and the environment

Human activity is anything that people do to get the things they need. How they do this is different, depending on where they live.

In some places people live very simply.

Egypt

Senegal

▲ In many parts of the world people still grow their own food.

▲ In **remote** areas people build their own homes and may not have electricity or running water.

In other places there is more human activity. In modern societies many people choose to live in a town or city.

In these places many homes are built and there needs to be piped water and a supply of energy, such as electricity. People need to travel for different reasons. Resources, including food, have to be brought into the city.

▲ Human activity has brought change to many countries in the Gulf region, as shown here in Dubai.

Human activity can very quickly damage or destroy the natural environment.

Everyone must use the things they have carefully. They should think about what to do with things they do not need or cannot use.

Activities

1 Work in a group to decide what human activity takes place in the area around your school or home.

2 Explain what you think is happening to the natural environment because of human activity.

3 Explain what people need to do to protect it.

In this lesson you will learn:
- about problems in the local environment
- about what can be done to take care of the local environment.

Threats to the environment

Litter and rubbish looks bad. Lots of it ends up in rivers and the sea.

▲ Rubbish that is not thrown away properly finds its way into the sea.

Land and water are spoiled when chemicals, oil, rubbish and human waste enter them. We say they are **polluted**.

The air is polluted by fumes from cars and other vehicles, from factories and power stations.

Taking resources from the natural environment can cause damage.

People can use the things they have carelessly. This means that more things need to be made, which uses more resources.

▲ Cars and other vehicles make fumes that go into the air.

Caring for the environment

Taking care of the natural environment is everybody's responsibility.

Everyone should learn about what they can do to help.

▲ When people have finished using a piece of land they can return it to a natural state.

Activity

Work in a small group. Make a poster that tells people three ways to cut down on their use of electricity.

4.11 Waste and recycling

In these lessons you will learn:

- about what waste is created
- about what can be done with waste
- about reducing, recycling and re-using waste.

What is waste?

We produce waste when we have things we no longer need or things we cannot use.

Food waste

Food waste happens because some parts of food plants and animals cannot be eaten, such as the skins and stems of some fruits and vegetables. Food waste is also a problem when people buy more than they need and it goes off before they can eat it.

Waste from food packaging

Today many foods and drinks come in cartons, plastic bottles, tins and cans.

◀ When things are thrown away, most of them end up in **landfill sites**.

Worn out waste

Some of the things we have wear out or break. When this happens we want to 'throw them away'.

Did you know?
A plastic bottle will last for about 450 years in a landfill site.

◀ A huge amount of bottled water is drunk in cities across Gulf countries.

What can be done?

People can reduce the waste they create by buying less to begin with.

Some items can be re-used a number of times or in different ways.

Many materials can be recycled. This means they are used again to make a new item.

▲ To help with recycling, materials need to be sorted into groups, such as plastics, metals, glass, cardboard and paper.

Activities

1 Work in a group. Think of three ways to re-use a plastic bottle or parts of one.

2 Write about what can be made from recycled paper, card and metal.

4.12 Managing money

In this lesson you will learn:
- that money comes from different sources
- that money can be used for different purposes
- about making choices when managing money.

What is money?

Money comes as coins and notes. We can exchange money for the things we need.

▲ We buy many things we need from shops and market stalls.

Where does money come from?

Most people work to earn money. Workers give their time, skills, effort and energy in exchange for money.

Pocket money

Many children get pocket money from their parents. This is often a set amount of money that children get each week. Sometimes children can earn more money. They get this if they do some extra work at home or do well in school.

▲ Some children earn pocket money by doing extra chores.

What can you do with money?

We can spend money. We buy the things we need and do things we enjoy.

We can also save money. Saving money means we do not spend all we have but put some in a safe place.

We might save money so that we can buy something expensive or so that we can use it in the future.

Activity

Make a four-part picture story about pocket money. You should show:

○ an adult at work

○ a child doing a simple chore

○ a child being paid pocket money

○ and the child doing something with that pocket money.

Label your drawings to say what each one shows.

4.13 Household spending

Household needs

People who live in the same dwelling make up a household. These people have needs that must be met every day. They need food, water, clothes and rest.

They also need energy, furniture and places to cook, wash and relax.

▲ Many modern homes provide for family entertainment.

Household spending

Some of the money earned by people in a household has to be spent on providing the things the household needs every day.

74

A household may also need to buy more expensive things. If the household cannot **afford** the expensive item, then some of the money a household has is saved. When the household has saved up enough money, the expensive items can be bought.

Sometimes households save money in case they need to spend money in the future on things they did not expect, such as repairing a house.

◀ A household manages money so that expensive items can be bought.

A household budget

A budget is a way of working out the money you have, how much of it you need to spend on different things and how much you want to save.

Activities

1 Make a list of the everyday things bought in your household in a week.

2 Draw three things a household might have to save up for.

Unit 4 Review questions

1 When we have certain duties or should behave in a certain way, these are our:
   a rights
   b achievements
   c responsibilities
   d hobbies

2 Written rules that are used in a country are called:
   a laws
   b sentences
   c responsibilities
   d duties

3 Greeting the people we meet is part of:
   a obeying rules
   b studying at school
   c showing good manners
   d being healthy

4 When the land, water or air are spoiled or made dirty, we say they are:
   a untidy
   b polluted
   c empty
   d wasted

5 Describe two ways in which you can look after the things you use in school.

6 Give three examples of things that need to be brought into a city for the people who live there.

7 Give two reasons why people create food waste.

8 Write two materials you think can be recycled and give one example of what they are used to make.

9 Name three things that a family has to buy to meet the needs of the family members.

10 Describe one expensive thing a family might buy and explain why they might buy it.

5 Health and wellbeing

In this unit you will learn:
- how to store food safely
- why exercise and sleep are important
- how to play safely
- to make a poster to inform people.

? Which of the things you do during the day use a lot of your energy?

physical effort
energy   exercise
fresh food

5.1 Keeping food safely

In these lessons you will learn:
- why food needs to be stored carefully
- how food can be preserved.

Fresh food

Fresh food needs to be eaten or cooked quite soon after it is bought.

Some foods become dry if they are not used quickly.

Some foods, especially vegetables and fruit, become soft and lose 'goodness'.

Unused fresh food finally goes stale or rotten.

▲ Old food can have mould growing on it and germs inside that can make us unwell.

Storing food

Different foods are stored in a variety of ways.

Some foods need to be kept in a cool, dry and dark place.

Some foods need to be kept cold, in a refrigerator.

Many foods are best kept in an airtight container.

Knowing how to store food properly helps us to avoid waste.

Preserving food

Preserving food means doing something to the food so that it can be kept for longer. People have been using different ways of preserving food for thousands of years. It can be preserved by being smoked, dried, cooked and put in jars or tins or frozen.

▲ Fresh foods like milk, meat and vegetables keep well in a refrigerator.

◄ These are two ways of preserving food.

Activities

1 Draw items of fresh food people will often buy and write how each one should be stored.

2 Work in a group to prepare an illustrated list of foods that are preserved in some way.

In these lessons you will learn:
- about germs and how they are spread
- when we need to clean our hands
- the five steps of cleaning hands.

Germs

Germs are tiny living things. Scientists call them microbes.

Some microbes help us by digesting our food.

▲ Special microbes help to make food like bread and yoghurt.

Some microbes are not good. If they get into our body they can make us ill. We usually call microbes that make us ill 'germs'.

◀ When some types of germs get into our body they make us ill.

Germs live on our bodies and especially on our hands.

We clean our hands so that we do not help germs get into our bodies.

We need to clean other parts of our body where germs might collect.

When should we wash our hands?

We need to wash our hands when:

- we have used the bathroom
- we have played outside
- we cough or sneeze
- we have visited a sick person
- we have touched an animal
- we are about to eat.

How do we wash our hands?

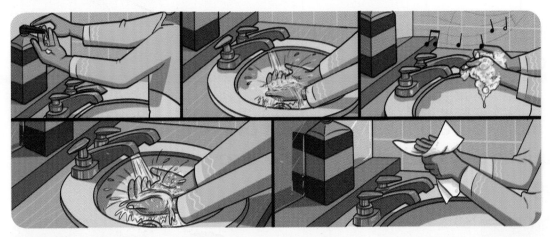

▲ There are a few simple steps to learn so that we wash our hands properly. How long should you scrub? For as long as it takes you to sing 'Happy Birthday to you'!

Staying healthy

We want to stay healthy because it is much better for us. When we are healthy we can do all the things we need to.

By keeping clean we do not spread germs which might make someone else ill.

Activities

1 Discuss with a partner all the things you could not do if you were ill in bed.

2 Work in a group to make a list of all the things in class that lots of people touch.

5.3 Exercise and rest

In these lessons you will learn:
- why your body needs exercise
- why your body needs rest.

Exercise

The food we eat gives us energy. We use some of the energy to grow and fight illness. We use energy to move.

We move in many different ways. If we move in a way that requires **physical effort** then we say we are exercising.

▲ Exercising helps our heart and muscles to stay strong.

Exercise uses up some of the energy we get from food. If we do not use up all this energy we can put on weight.

Rest and sleep

When we feel tired we know we need some sleep.

▲ Our bodies need to rest and to sleep.

Sleeping helps our body relax and repair any injuries.

If we sleep well, we have more energy. We remember more, can concentrate longer and pay closer attention. We can also think more clearly.

If we do not get enough sleep we are more likely to be in a bad mood, to be clumsy and to find our work difficult.

▲ As well as sleeping, we sometimes need to rest during the day.

Activities

1 In a group, discuss the movements you make throughout the day. List them in order with the ones that use the most energy first and the ones that use least energy last.

2 Work in a group. Make a poster about the importance of getting enough sleep.

5.4 Playing safely

In these lessons you will learn:
- about some dangers we meet every day
- where we can play safely
- how to play safely.

Avoiding danger

We are safe most of the time. There is always a chance that we can be hurt.

We can be hurt by falling off something, falling into something, falling over something or by something falling on us.

We can be hurt if something hits or cuts us.

We can get a shock from electricity.

Some chemicals can cause burns and others are poisonous.

▲ We should never play near traffic.

Where can we play safely?

If we need to find a place to play, then we need to see if it is well away from any dangers like traffic.

Good places to play are playgrounds and parks.

▲ Playgrounds are great fun as long as we are sensible.

How can we play safely?

Playing should be fun. We can do some things to make sure we are as safe as possible when we play.

We have to be especially careful when we climb off the ground, when we are on something that is moving or if we are near water.

We need to wear suitable clothes for the activity and for the weather conditions.

◀ What do we need to think about if we are playing out in the sunshine?

We should never play alone.

It is always good to have an adult that we know with us.

Activities

1 Draw a playground and label all the dangers.

2 Work in a group to make a poster showing different ways to play safely in a park.

1 If fresh food is not used quickly it:
   a tastes better
   b has more goodness in it
   c can go stale or rotten
   d looks more delicious

2 A special word for germs is:
   a organs
   b diseases
   c microbes
   d infections

3 When we exercise we:
   a move in a way that requires extra physical effort
   b sit or lie in a relaxed position
   c try to keep our body very still
   d breathe slowly

4 Making sure that I am safe while I play is mostly:
   a my parents' responsibility
   b my friends' responsibility
   c my teacher's responsibility
   d my responsibility

5 Describe two ways in which food can be preserved.

6 Describe two ways in which germs can be spread between people in a classroom.

7 Describe what needs to happen if germs are going to be able to make us ill.

8 Describe the different stages of cleaning your hands properly.

9 Explain two ways in which exercise is good for you.

10 Describe two benefits of having a proper amount of rest and sleep.

Glossary

afford to have enough money to be able to pay for something

aim to have an aim is to try to bring something about or make something happen, as in 'my team aims to win the game'

built-up an area where many people live and there are man-made features such as houses, roads and offices

concrete a building material made from broken stones, sand, cement and water

continent one of the world's main continuous areas of land

contribution a part played by someone towards a common aim

culture a way of life, the way a group of people does certain things. Culture is passed on through beliefs, practices, clothes, food and art

gadgets a small electronic or mechanical item, usually able to do something new or to do something in a new way

generations all the members of a family who are of a similar age

globe a model of the Earth with a map on the surface

goal the end result of some effort, what is hoped will be achieved

heritage valued cultural traditions and historic buildings passed down from earlier times and generations

industry human activity where different things are made or services are given

ingredients foods and other items put together to make a dish of food

key a table used to explain the symbols on a map

landfill site a large hole dug in the ground where solid waste is dumped and eventually covered over

manners the way a person behaves towards others

marriage a legal union of a man and a woman

physical effort the body using energy to move itself or something

polluted spoilt with fumes, chemicals, oil or rubbish

remote a remote area is a place a long way from any other settlement or human activity

responsibilities duties which require us to do something or to behave in a certain way

society a large group, usually within a country's boundaries, that shares common ideas

steel a hard, strong, grey metal

symbols a shape used to show something on a map

technology using science to help in business, industry or in the home

timeline a way of showing events in order of when they happened, along a line

traditional a way of thinking, behaving or doing something that has been used by a group of people for a very long time